How Big Is Your
Umbrella?

How Big Is Your
Umbrella?

Weathering the Storms of Life

Sheila Wray Gregoire

ISBN: 978-1-4866-0004-5

Word Alive Press
131 Cordite Road, Winnipeg, MB R3W 1S1
www.wordalivepress.ca

WORD ALIVE PRESS
Just Write!

Cataloguing in Publication information may be obtained through Library and Archives Canada

Contents

Introduction

I often wish life were more like a fairy tale—we may spend a few days battling dragons or evil stepmothers or wicked kings, but our happily ever after is just around the corner. And we expect the happily ever after. We deserve the happily ever after. So why doesn't God give it to us?

Jesus told us a story two thousand years ago about two men who wanted to settle down. One man focused on prime waterfront real estate and built his house on the beach, dreaming of an idyllic life of fishing and swimming. Another man, eyeing the incoming tide, moved inland and built his house anchored on rock. Soon a storm hit, and as the wind and the rain battered the houses, only one stood firm.

Storms come to everyone—that's the way life works. The only difference is in our preparation. We build our house securely by making God the foundation of our lives. No matter what happens, we do not bend or break or collapse because God holds us. When we look to Him despite the circumstances, the storms lose their power.

Yet turning to God is not always easy. Sometimes storms wail against us so strongly that standing through them isn't possible. We are knocked down and need help getting back up when the waves are crashing over us.

I think that during those awful times, God desperately wants to come to our rescue. He's standing out in the storm with us, reaching out His hand. But will we take it? Sometimes we're hesitant, because we don't understand the storm. Did God cause it? Why isn't it going away? What does He want from us? The questions beat us down almost as much as the wind and the rain, and we feel hopeless, powerless, and, all too often, alone.

Throughout my life I, like you, have faced a myriad of storms. As I recount my story here, and weave in those of others, I hope to show you that there is indeed hope. If you are worn down and you can't get up, there is no pit you can dig where God cannot still reach you and pull you up. If you have lost your passion for life and the world seems gray, it can burst with color again. Don't despair. God is with us, and a rainbow awaits.

1

We Cry:
"What Did I Do to
Deserve This?"

When storms come, frequently our first reaction is to lash out at God. "Why me?" "Why don't You do something?" "Why are You letting this happen?"

Throughout recorded history, when people have walked through really tough times, they have taken it up with their Maker. The prophet Jeremiah, seeing the slaughter of his people, yelled at God, "Why does the way of the wicked prosper?" (Jer. 12:1). In his psalms, King David lamented and even raged about the injustices all around him and what he had to endure. Both David and Jeremiah eventually did make peace with their questions and with God, but the wailing came first.

I have done my own share of wailing at God over loss, rejections, and hurts. The deepest occurred when I was twenty-six and pregnant with my second child. The day after my sonogram, everything seemed to move in slow motion after the phone rang and the doctor said, "You'd better come in, because there's something wrong with his heart."

Over the next few weeks, as I had every test imaginable, my husband and I learned that our son had Down syndrome and a serious heart defect that would require a series of surgeries. These operations, however, would only prolong his death, not save his life. The doctors couldn't be certain when he would leave us, but they did believe that he would deteriorate, grow very short of breath, and suffer until he finally died, whether it be as a baby, a toddler, or a twenty-year-old.

I felt like a shadow of my former self as I walked through the last half of my pregnancy in trepidation and cold, brutal terror. When Christopher arrived on August 6, 1996, it was such a relief to finally see him. He was no longer an abstract medical problem, but a tiny bundle who breathed a little too fast, and who stared directly into my eyes as if he knew who I was.

His first two weeks were peaceful ones, as he was healthier than we expected him to be. We were praying that he could avoid surgery, and that he might even improve on his own, but God did not answer that prayer as we would have liked. As his heart began to fail, Christopher grew increasingly tired and lost weight. The surgery was his only hope, even though the doctors gave that only a 25 percent chance of success. By that time he was down to four pounds, far too small for the ordeal that lay ahead of him.

On the morning of his operation, when I handed him over to the anesthetist, I was terrified I would never hold him again. But the surgery went well, and the doctors grew optimistic about his chances. Five days later, however, Christopher's breathing again grew rapid. That night my mother watched our daughter, Rebecca, so that my husband, Keith, and I could visit our son together. "Mommy loves you, sweetheart," I whispered as we left his room.

Christopher was only twenty-nine days old when he died later that night. I had never known what it was for a heart to truly break until that moment.

C. S. Lewis, after the death of his wife, remarked that grief felt a lot like fear. It produced the same sickening pit in your stomach that preceded something truly awful. That's what I felt over the next few days, too. But what was it, exactly, that I was afraid of? Waking up the next morning and dealing with the loss again? Facing the future alone? Forgetting? Going crazy? That God really is malicious? Or that the feeling would never end?

Perhaps it was a combination of them all. After Christopher's death, I was scared simultaneously of recovering so quickly I'd forget him, and of never being able to cope again. In the middle of this turmoil, I wailed many questions at God to try to make sense out of what was happening. In many ways, though, this quest was self-serving. I reasoned that if I could just find the reason for this storm, if I could just figure out what God was doing, He'd stop. I could move on. This pain would end, or at least the coping could begin. So I searched my repertoire of explanations for suffering in order to make sense of it. And as I did, I cried out these questions.

Is God Trying to Teach Me Something?

About a decade before my son's illness, my mother was diagnosed with breast cancer. The surgeon believed, based on the size and type of tumor, that it had already spread, and that her time was short. I remember sitting alone, in shock, as my mother lay in the hospital, thinking that this must be happening because I hadn't been reading my Bible enough. I believed that God was trying to get my attention.

Thankfully, my mother recovered, as did my devotional diligence. But were these two things really causally related? It's easy to dismiss such adolescent musings now, but many adults entertain a similar thought: the reason the storm is raging is because God will use anything at His disposal to make His point. When Christopher died, my husband and I received some condolence cards by well-meaning people who wrote such things as, "Smile through this. God is teaching you something. Rejoice that He has chosen this route to show you what that is!"

Besides being a very insensitive thing to say to a grieving parent, I'm not even sure that this presents a true picture of the origin of our storms or the way that God intends for us to react. First, the insinuation is that the reason this hurricane is blowing is because God wants to get our attention. It's for our own good, because God loves us. And if it's for our own good, then we had better smile, as if it really isn't so bad. Shouldn't we be grateful that God is reaching out to teach us, we who are obviously so unteachable that God had to send *this*?

Let me turn this question in another direction. Is there any evidence that this was Jesus' attitude to pain and suffering? After all, when Jesus' friends died, Jesus wept. When Herod had John the Baptist murdered, Jesus went away by Himself (Matt. 14:13). He even wrestled in prayer for what His disciples would have to endure (John 17:6–19). Jesus felt the pain that we all experience as part of life, and He didn't try to deny the reality of that pain by saying, "It's all for your good." Even when it was for our good—when Lazarus was raised so that we could see Jesus' power (John 11:14–15, 39–40)—He *still* wept! Feeling grief is not denying God's goodness in our lives; it's being true to our humanity.

But even if storms are legitimate occasions for grief, does God still send horrible events to lead us to Him? Throughout the Old Testament, the nation of Israel was punished because they did not listen to God. However, this only happened after Israel had been told repeatedly what to do and had ignored these warnings. Destruction certainly wasn't God's first choice of ways for making His point. When Jesus wanted to teach people something, what did He do? Instead of inflicting suffering, He often retreated with them for some one-on-one time. He laughed with them, listened to them, entered into their lives. He showed them love. While He did rebuke the Pharisees on a number of occasions, His modus operandi was to woo with love, not to zap with lightning. There are times when God sends hardships to call people back to Him, but this seems to be the exception, not the rule.

Of course, storms are excellent growth opportunities. As James told us, "The testing of your faith develops perseverance" (James 1:3). Looking back I can see that blessing in my own life. Just because we can ultimately benefit from storms, though, does not always mean that a spiritual deficiency *caused* the storm in the first place. Nor will learning a spiritual truth necessarily end the storm, as much as we would like it to. We may want a nice, pat explanation for our suffering, but there's probably more going on than a simple spiritual lesson.

What Did I Do to Cause This?

It's only a small step from feeling that God is trying to teach us something to feeling that we must be the cause of the catastrophe. We reason that if God is trying to get through to us, it's likely because He's angry. This must be His punishment, at least at some level. What makes this line of thinking especially devastating is that if God is angry, we feel separated from Him. We can't run to Him. The only real source of help we have during storms now feels cut off from us.

But just because we are suffering, it doesn't necessarily mean that we have done something wrong; often it's the exact opposite! When Peter was writing to the persecuted church, he said, ". . . if you endure when you do right and suffer for it, you have God's approval" (1 Peter 2:20 NRSV). God may not be angry at all; He may be proud!

Nevertheless, there are certainly times when we don't feel God's approval during storms. Let's assume for a minute that we actually did something to cause a storm, or at least to aggravate it. Does that mean we are beyond God's help? Does it mean that He is so angry or disappointed that he leaves us floundering on our own? Remember, Jesus says, "Come to me, all you who are weary and burdened, and I will give you rest" (Matt. 11:28).

If you feel some responsibility for your storms, you may find this invitation really hard to accept. Author Donna Mann was led into a grief-counseling ministry through her own tragedy. Her two-year-old daughter escaped through a door Donna didn't know the toddler could open, and drowned in the family's swimming pool. Though Donna obviously never intended for it to happen, the accusation was always there: if you had been a conscientious mother, your daughter would still be alive. For years, these accusations—as well as regrets of things unsaid—prevented Donna from working through her grief. She simply stood in the middle of the storm until she became accustomed to it.

Sadly, many of us find it hard to run to God for shelter because we feel like we deserve the storm. If only I had been a better wife. If only I had spent more time with my kids when I had the chance. If only I had wanted my baby all along. If only I had locked that door. If only I had said this or that. We feel as if we have no right to recover from the storm because we were to blame for it. We can't mourn what we lost because we didn't appreciate it enough in the first place. Guilt is making our storms worse. We can't walk through to the other side.

For Donna, as for many of us, seeing God's perspective through the fog of guilt is difficult. When we're angry with ourselves, we usually project that anger onto Him. He must be angry too. Whenever the guilt hits full force, so does the feeling that condemnation is raining down on us from heaven.

Of course, Donna's problem was not sin, since in her case it was an accident. But what if we are guilty of doing something blatantly wrong? What should our storm plan be then?

Sin certainly does anger God, but that does not mean His anger keeps us from healing. Quite the contrary! If God's desire is to make us like Christ (see Rom. 8:29), then He wants to give us power and motivation to change, not to zap all of our energy by condemning us in perpetuity. In Jeremiah 15:19, God says, "If you repent, I will restore you that you may serve me." When God convicts us of a specific sin, He does so to help us join His mission once again. He does not do so to cast us out. His conviction calls us home, back to shelter, where we can thrive again.

If your feelings of guilt have left you standing alone in the storm, then your guilt is likely not from God. Guilt attacks us as persons. It says we don't deserve to live. It says we don't deserve to be happy, and that we didn't deserve the happiness we once experienced from the loved one we lost, the job before it turned sour, or our health before we were struck down. It whispers words of despair. Conviction, on the other hand, looks at our deeds and offers a way out and a way back to the God who accepts and loves us.

One of the most important breakthroughs that helped Donna through the storm was the realization that she could still have a relationship with her daughter through her memories, as painful as they were. She couldn't change the events of that fateful morning, but those events did not invalidate the two wonderful years she had experienced with her child. In fact, characterizing the relationship solely on the basis of that one moment poisoned the whole history of it. When she went to God, she was given the gift of seeing the big picture again.

Don't let guilt rob you of the comfort God offers or the perspective He wants to give you. The Bible says, "Cast all your anxiety on him because he cares for you" (1 Peter 5:7). No matter what you have done, God cares. Don't deny yourself His shelter.

Who Is the Storm Really About?

Trying to figure out what God is teaching us or how we're to blame are common reactions to storms, even though they often block us from the comfort He longs to give. But there's another fundamental problem with these reactions. Think about these questions: What do I need to learn? What did I do to deserve this? How could I have caused this? Do you notice how all of them center around "I"?

When Christopher was ill, I remember talking to our minister about him. Trying to appear very spiritual, I said, "I just want to learn whatever God is trying to show me." My pastor then said something that absolutely floored me. "Why do you assume any of this has anything to do with you?"

What did he mean? Of course it had to do with me—Christopher was my son! Nothing had ever affected me this much. And yet, the beginning of a nagging doubt was born: perhaps I was asking the wrong questions.

In 1964, Helen Roseveare served as a missionary doctor in the Congo. When that nation erupted in a coup, rebels captured her along with other female missionaries. Over the next few months, she endured beatings, rape, and other horrors. During one of the most degrading experiences, Helen remembers the question God whispered in her mind: "Can you thank me for trusting you with this, even if I never tell you why?" Suddenly Helen realized that God was in control. Even if she never saw the fruits, she was part of a plan that went far beyond her.

History is filled with examples of people who endured horrendous storms because God was accomplishing something bigger through them. Think how the suffering of Martin Luther King, Jr., the martyrs of the early church, or even the Allied soldiers in World War II helped make the world better, though at great personal cost. Maybe you can't see God's purposes now. Joseph certainly didn't when he was sold into slavery by his brothers and then spent years in prison for something he didn't do (see Gen. 37, 39–40). Maybe you will never see what God is doing on this side of heaven. But you are part of the story that God is writing.

In my own life, I have seen how God has used Christopher's death in many ways, but there are other things I have not seen, and never will with my earthly eyes. They're still being worked out. God trusted Keith and me with our precious son, and He continues to trust us today. In 1 Corinthians 10:13, Paul writes that God never puts something in our path that is too difficult for us. He always provides a way of escape, a way through the storm. You can find that way by relying on Him.

When my pastor challenged my assumptions, it was as if God was finally pulling me out of the howling wind and back toward shelter. I had had everything backward. I hadn't realized that in trying to find answers I was actually walking further into the storm, rather than closer to God. I thought God wanted me to seek out *reasons,* when what He really wanted me to do was to seek out *Himself.* So, is trying to find spiritual lessons in our storms wrong? Not at all! But painting this as the will behind the storm paints a picture of a God that is mean-spirited and much smaller than the God we find in Scripture.

The reasons may or may not be revealed, as Helen Roseveare

found, but God is still there. He is the One who would provide the shelter, the way of escape, the hope and will and power to keep us clinging to the offered branch. We may never know the reasons, but we can know God and rest in Him. Storms may be bigger than us, but they're not bigger than Him. As we seek Him, we will receive His wonderful promises: we will learn, we will grow in holiness, and we will develop perseverance. We can fully accept these promises not when we condemn ourselves, but when we trust God no matter what may come.

Looking for reasons for the storms is only natural. But as we voice our questions, yelling into the wind, God is simultaneously calling us toward shelter. Even if we never understand why, He is the one in control, He has trusted us with this, and He will carry us through. That is our promise, our shelter, and our comfort.

2

We Cry: "Why Does God Let Me Suffer?"

Knowing that God is at the center of our suffering is a good starting point, but it doesn't stop the questions, does it? In fact, it may even make some worse. If all of this is happening not necessarily as a punishment or even primarily as a spiritual lesson, then that means God is letting it happen without even considering me! What kind of a God is that? What kind of a God would send storms that knock us over, that steal the very air we breathe, that crush us under their power? Why would He allow such suffering?

How Does God Feel About Suffering?

Before we try to answer that, let's get a picture of how God feels when we do suffer. If He's upset by it, too, that has the potential to change our perspective, doesn't it? I think our best clues about how God feels can be found in how His Son handled hardships on this earth. In His time on earth, Jesus wept when Lazarus died, and He was consumed by what He knew Jerusalem was going to suffer after

His death. Jesus felt things very deeply. Perhaps one of the reasons was that death was never supposed to be part of His creation, and such suffering may wound His Spirit even more than it does ours. He alone can envision what life would have been like—indeed, should have been like—had we not sinned and brought evil into the world. When Adam and Eve ate the fruit and disobeyed God, they didn't just throw a wall up between themselves and God. The world itself changed. Illness and pain came. Weeds and devouring insects came. Paradise was lost. And God was not happy about it, just as He is not happy when we face storms today.

When I first heard that my son would likely die, I was devastated. I remember running outside without a coat to have it out with God one cold, gray April day. As tears streamed down my face, I accused God. "I don't understand," I yelled. "How do you expect me to watch my only son die?"

And then, in the middle of the wind and the rain, I heard a small voice saying to my spirit, "I know, Sheila. I know. I did it too."

It was the first time I understood a bit of what it must have been like for God to watch His Son die. For some reason, it had never seemed real to me that Jesus' agony would be difficult for God to endure, since the cross had, after all, been His plan all along. And yet God watched Jesus be tortured and betrayed and humiliated and torn apart, all because He loved us that much and wanted a relationship with us. God understood and felt my pain, and I knew He was going to carry me through.

Why Doesn't God Protect Me?

God shows over and over that He grieves when His children are hurting. And you are His child! But this poses a big conundrum for us when we are suffering, especially when the storm involves something that was done to us by another. After all, human parents usually try to protect their kids. That's why children run to Mommy and Daddy in the middle of the storm. It's not that they believe Mommy and Daddy will stop the storm; it's because they know they are safe with them, because parents will give anything to protect you. They are fierce on your behalf.

So why wasn't God fierce for you? Why didn't He stop the hurt? Perhaps our human eyes cause us to miss what is really occurring. Jesus reserved His sternest warnings for those who would hurt children. He told the crowds: "If anyone causes one of these little ones who believe in me to sin, it would be better for him to have a large millstone hung around his neck and to be drowned in the depths of the sea" (Matt. 18:6). To those listening, that must have sounded strange. Children in those days had fewer rights than children do today. To Jesus' contemporaries, looking around them, there was no evidence that God would actually do what Jesus claimed. Yet there was a warning in what Jesus said: troublemakers such as these are in for it. There will be an accounting. Just as it's not a good idea to get between a mother bear and her cubs, it's not a good idea to get between God and one of the children He loves. We may wish to see that accounting now, but know that it is coming, and that God will ultimately do battle for you.

Is God Waiting to Hurt Me?

No matter how God Himself reacts to the storm, though, the thought is probably still with us: Why did God allow it in the first place? After all, He could just quiet the winds around us, just as He quieted the waters two thousand years ago. So why doesn't He take the pain away, bring my wife back, heal my child, strike down my abuser? We want to understand. We want justice. We want things fixed. Why doesn't God yield to our demands?

In Ecclesiastes 3:5, God says there is "a time to scatter stones and a time to gather them." Sometimes our dreams do come crashing down. Sometimes the stones, those things that we have built our lives with, are scattered. Just as victims are shown on TV the day after the hurricane, standing amid the wreckage of what used to be their homes, so we are left, forlorn, to sift through what remains of our lives.

Does this mean that God deliberately causes this scattering? Not always. The Old Testament provides the classic case of suffering unplanned by God. Job was an upright man. Satan asked God's permission to prove that Job wouldn't really stay faithful to God if times got tough. God gave it. As a result, Job suffered tremendous tragedy. Satan stripped him of all that he had, but Job stayed true to God. And Job wasn't the only one who experienced such a thing. Jesus told Peter that Satan had asked to "sift [Peter] as wheat" (Luke 22:31). Even though Jesus prayed for Peter, clearly God okayed it. Suffering may not necessarily reflect God's plans as much as it reflects another battle waging unseen.

But even if a storm wasn't God's idea, He still allowed it to happen, didn't He? God doesn't have to say yes to any storm, but He sometimes does. Doesn't He understand how much that can hurt us? And when storms seem to run counter to what we think God's will is, it's especially hurtful and difficult to understand. How do we cope when a marriage God blessed breaks up and we're left picking up the pieces with our children? How do we reconcile with God when church communities fall apart so that His work can no longer be done? Why would God want such things to be demolished around our feet? Why wouldn't He step in and rescue?

God knew these questions would plague us, and so He preempted them. Over 2,500 years ago, God told us through the prophet Jeremiah: "'For I know the plans I have for you,' declares the LORD, 'plans to prosper you and not to harm you, plans to give you hope and a future'" (Jer. 29:11). That is how God sees you, your spouse, your children, your friends. He is not waiting to hurt them. He has plans to give them a future and hope, and to give you hope, too.

God doesn't stop at telling us that we should have hope, though. He also includes that little phrase—"and not to harm you"—to reassure us. He wouldn't have thrown that in unless that fear was real to many of us. Deep down, we are afraid that God really does want to harm us. But God says, in no uncertain terms, that He does not. Sometimes bad things will happen, but that does not mean we have no hope or no future.

This doesn't always make sense when we look around and see all the scattered stones. When Christopher was diagnosed, it was as if any hope for his life was taken away. He wouldn't have a future. So how could this verse even apply to him? For that matter, how could the verse apply to a young mom diagnosed with terminal cancer? If there is no hope and no future, how does this even make sense?

Perhaps we misunderstand the nature of hope. Think of the story of Joni Eareckson Tada, who was paralyzed from the neck down after a diving accident when she was 17. I'm sure her parents hoped great things for her. When she was paralyzed, it looked like those things couldn't happen. But all was not lost! God kept Joni close to Him. He comforted her, wooed her, filled her, and, best of all, used her. Isn't that the real hope?

The promise of hope can take us beyond the question of "why" that seems inherent in suffering. It has been said that hope is faith directed toward the future. Hope is to live as if we know something unknowable. It is to believe that God will use our children, our illness, our financial difficulties, even if He never reveals how or why. Hope operates on a different timeline. While we think in the here and now, hope looks to God's promise that He does have a good plan for this world. Hope, then, is submitting what we want to God's sovereignty.

While Jeremiah assured us that God doesn't deliberately hurt us, the apostle Paul went even further. Romans 8:28 says, "We know that in all things God works for the good of those who love him." Notice that Paul does not say that all things *are* good. A child's death in a car accident is not good; a young mother dying of breast cancer is not good; my son's death was not good. To say so is grotesque. But while these situations are not good, God can bring good out of them. We may never know why something happened on this earth, but we can take comfort that God will bring good out of even our deepest pain. The bad does not have to be the end of the story.

How Can I Cope with This Fear?

Knowing that God will bring good can be comforting in the long run, but coping in the here and now can still be excruciating. What do we do when we're stuck in the middle, when we can't see the good He promises, and when we may not even know how or when the storm will end? The waiting—and the not knowing—is often harder than dealing with the finality of the devastation after the storm has passed.

When Christopher was first diagnosed with a heart problem, the doctors left so much up in the air. At every appointment, we were given one more possible scenario. No one could be sure what would actually happen, and I felt like I had to go over and over each scenario in my mind, so that no matter what happened, I would be prepared. In the end, however, all the possibilities I had envisioned failed to materialize. I had to endure something unanticipated. I wasted all that time worrying when I could have been praying, trusting, or resting.

Fear is a normal human response to the unknown. Think about how many times God tells us not to be afraid. The first words spoken by the angels announcing Jesus' birth were "do not be afraid." To John, receiving the revelation, Jesus said the same thing. In fact, it's a pattern in the Bible: whenever people get a heavenly visitation, they're petrified. The closer we come to an encounter with God, the scarier life can be!

However, it does not follow that life is somehow *worse*. Fear can also accompany the greatest heights we ever reach. Peter had to cast aside his own fears in order to do something incredible. In Matthew 14, we read that Peter, along with the other disciples, was cowering on a boat during a storm when he saw Jesus walking toward them— on the water. Peter asked to come out, and Jesus called him. Despite his fear, Peter went over the edge of the boat. He took Jesus' hand and actually walked! But then he let the waves and the wind distract him, and he floundered and started to sink.

When we recount that story, we frequently focus on Peter's failure, but perhaps that's the wrong perspective. After all, as far as we know he is one of only two people who have ever successfully walked on water. And he did so even though he was frightened. His fears weren't banished entirely. It was just that when he looked at Jesus, fear took a back seat.

I think that's what overcoming fear looks like. It's not displaying bravado; it's moving forward even though we're scared. That requires us to let God be our focus, not the fear. That's the hard part, because fear has this nasty habit of consuming our attention. And whether we're looking inside us or around us, there's one place we're not looking: up at Jesus. When I heard God say to me, "I know how it feels to watch your son die. I did too," I believe He was telling me, "I understand. You don't have to go through this alone. Rest in me." He was changing my focus from my problems, which seemed insurmountable, to God, who could carry me.

What Does It Mean to Trust God?

Focusing on God instead of our fears boils down to an issue of trust. Do we trust God to look after what is dear to us, and especially *who* is dear to us? When we clutch those we love tightly, we try to take control, rather than letting God have it. We don't believe in God's hope.

Nevertheless, it can be terribly difficult to believe that God is worthy of our trust, especially when circumstances seem to tell us loudly and clearly that God isn't acting in a trustworthy manner. Yet some of the most incredible stories of hope are not those where the circumstances are rosy, but those where people rise above their circumstances.

What does it look like if we replace our fear with the hope God promises? Hope isn't like a rabbit's foot. It doesn't involve crossing our fingers and holding our breath and jumping through hoops for God. When I was pregnant with Christopher, I strove to have enough hope that God would heal him. I read all the Scriptures that related to healing, and focused on the verse: "If you have faith and do not doubt, . . . it will be done" (Matt. 21:21). So I worked myself up to have that kind of faith. I never let myself think about what would happen if my son didn't make it—that would mean that I didn't have faith! I would go to each ultrasound, each checkup, believing that he would be healed. When he wasn't, I was sure it was because I didn't have enough faith.

In talking to other families enduring terrible crises, I found this reaction to bad news quite common. Recently, I encountered a family whose child was in the final stages of cancer. It was clear that she didn't have much time left. Yet the family prayed every day, thanking God for the healing she was about to receive. They e-mailed updates about Scriptures that God had used to comfort them overnight, about how she would be healed. They held healing services at her bedside. Their older children wrote songs about the healing that was to come. Their whole faith was focused toward this little girl recovering.

Is this the faith Jesus was talking about in Matthew 21? This family felt that if they could just have enough belief, God would have to heal. Trusting God, however, does not mean having faith that God will let everything turn out the way we want it to turn out. Trusting God means having faith *even if* things don't turn out the way we want them to.

Having faith is letting God make the decisions, not you. Ironically, allowing God *not* to heal sometimes exhibits more faith than working yourself up to believe beyond a shadow of a doubt that He will heal. When you do not dictate the outcome of an illness, a job loss, or any other storm, you are allowing God to be in control. You say your hope is in God, not in what will unfold.

This is not to say that God does not heal, or that He does not ask us to claim His miracles in our lives. Cliff, a friend from church, had been suffering for two years from a lung illness that doctors could not diagnose. In a business meeting with a fellow Christian, the client asked if Cliff had claimed the promise God had given him years ago about the work He was going to do through his family's ministry. That night, Cliff called a family prayer meeting, and they claimed that promise. Cliff was immediately healed.

As much as we would like this story to be commonplace, miracles don't seem to happen very often. Jesus did not heal everyone, and all the apostles eventually died even though they had performed miraculous signs themselves. God allows horrible and unspeakable things. But He does not rejoice over them.

Having the hope that God promises through our trials, then, is not hope in *what* God will do as much as it is hope in *who* God is. The first question we asked—What did I do to deserve this?—brought us back to God. So, ultimately, does this question—Why does God let me suffer? God does not leave us to huddle in the storm alone. He ends with a promise: the storm, though it may be all you can see now, is not what will endure. The bad is never the end of the story. God is still writing the conclusion, and it is one full of hope, because it is also full of His love.

3

We Cry:
"Don't You Want Me to
Be Happy?"

To know that we have hope carves a path out of our deepest valleys, for it turns us to God even in hard times. Yet I still wailed at God, even when I accepted that God would ultimately bring good out of my situation. How can you not when your heart is being torn out? When I was particularly desperate, I would turn to the comforting passages in the Bible that said things like, "God loves to give good gifts to His children." I'd comfort myself with the thought that this must mean everything will turn out okay in the end. There's no need to worry; I just need to hang on.

If you've ever felt that way, you know what happens when things don't turn out okay. We turn up the volume at God: Don't you want me to be happy? After all, we know how things *should* turn out. We want healthy families, close relationships, financial security, a good job, outward signs of success. What could possibly be wrong with that? Isn't that what God wants for us too?

We believe we've found the recipe for success: follow God, and everything else will fall into place. And as Christians, so often that becomes our primary aim: to prove to God that we deserve His outward blessings so we can be happy.

I was vividly reminded of the value our culture places on happiness in the late 1980s when my mother took me on a trip to the Caribbean. It was supposed to be paradise, but there were two problems. First, outside our room resided two roosters who believed it was their job to ensure that everyone knew the precise moment that morning had broken. This wouldn't have been so bad had it not also been for the disco that was located right above us. Its DJ was in possession of only one song: "Don't Worry, Be Happy." Every night, as I lay awake listening to those insipid words, I grew more and more worried and less and less happy.

Why Happiness Hurts

"Be Happy" could be our generation's theme song. We live in a culture that seems to believe that the purpose of life is the elimination of all storms, and that is, indeed, how we define happiness. It's not an inner quality, like joy, but an outer state that's highly dependent on life going well. But this notion that life should be smooth sailing is a relatively new one. The only reason we entertain it is because it seems possible. Material wealth has eradicated many of the miseries people have endured over the centuries, and medical advances mean early death or disability are not as likely as they once were. There's no reason why we can't dedicate our lives to the "pursuit of happiness." When a storm comes, it's not seen as a natural course of events, but a betrayal. Pain is not to be tolerated.

And yet, for all our emphasis on happiness, we're a profoundly unhappy society. The rate of antidepressant use is staggering. We report ourselves to be more stressed, more lonely, more hopeless than previous generations. We're looking, but we're not finding.

Perhaps our search for happiness has actually hindered our ability to find it. I believe happiness is like a boomerang: if we aim for it, we're going to get whacked. As an example, think about what happens when the expectations of happiness and the experiences of parenthood collide. Many parents expect their children to make them happy by fulfilling their unmet needs. Now, finally, there will be someone to love me, stick by me, validate me. But children naturally rebel against this kind of pressure. The very desire for children to make you happy often pushes children away, and you end up unhappier than you were before.

The marriage relationship offers even more danger in the happiness department. We marry because we believe we've found our "perfect match." When happiness doesn't suddenly blossom, the fault must lie with the other person. Your spouse was supposed to complete you—but didn't—and now he needs to shape up. However, when we give in to this line of thinking, we place happiness outside of ourselves. We say, "I'll be happy when he finally spends time with us" or "I'll be happy when she finally appreciates what I do for the family." Our happiness is based on what someone else does. And if that person doesn't change, happiness remains unattainable.

If our source of happiness is external, we'll never find it. There will always be something we lack, or some way in which our lives aren't cutting it. When we look for something else—or someone else—to make us happy, we concentrate on whether that person is measuring up, not on whether we measure up. We're not interested in heart issues as much as in personal satisfaction. Perhaps this is one reason we find it so difficult to cope with storms today. Our self-worth, fulfillment, and peace have been placed outside of us and so can easily be snatched away.

To follow this to its logical extreme, it may sound as if I'm advocating, "Don't care about anything, and then you won't be hurt!" Yet that's not what God calls us to do. It's not that we shouldn't enjoy things. We just need to remember that they cannot fill an empty heart.

What's Better than Happiness?

In Jesus' list of blessings given during the Sermon on the Mount, many things were lauded other than happiness: meekness, peacemaking, hungering and thirsting after righteousness. Happiness, perhaps, is not the point.

But since our society is geared toward happiness, those of us who follow God are put in a difficult position when we're not happy. We may not want to base our emotional state on outward things, but it's only natural in our days of drive-through convenience, do-it-yourself projects, and keeping up with the Joneses. So we try to work through this dilemma of how God, who is supposed to love us, would allow us to be unhappy. In doing so, we frequently draw the analogy of a wise parent and an immature child to reconcile our circumstances with a God who loves us.

The reasoning goes something like this: God is a parent who simply wants what's best for us, but we're too dense to know what that is. God is in the same position that you might be if your child wanted to do something and you refused because you knew it wouldn't be good for him or her. Your reassurances that you have your child's well-being in mind doesn't stop her from saying, "If you really loved me, you'd understand how much this means to me!" These reassurances don't stop his temper tantrums or the slammed doors or the silent treatment. But you stick to your guns precisely because you do love your child.

Maybe this is how God is, we reason. He does things that we may not necessarily like because He knows what's best for us. Yet while there is some truth to this, this picture of God is still quite problematic, isn't it? I remember one missionary telling me that, after hearing the call to go overseas, she begged not to be sent to India, knowing full well that that's where God would send her. "I didn't want to go to India. I hated the idea of India. So, of course, God sent me there." She had a sense of humor about the whole episode, and came to love India in time, but I think many of us also have this cod-liver oil idea about God: whatever we hate most must be what's good for us, and that's what God will do.

Is this how we should understand storms? I don't think of God as an eat-your-liver-and-brussels-sprouts deity. He is a God who designed the festivals of the Israelites to be feasts, or parties, not the child sacrifices of the neighboring nations. Look at the world He created: it's full of vividly colored flowers and beautiful creatures, and laughter and fun. God pronounced all of this good. I think even children are indicative of God's perspective on fun. Children—human and animal—all seem to have a sense of play. Since fun is such a part of God's creation, we can't explain why God does not answer our pleas for happiness on the basis that God doesn't value fun. Of course, we also can't say that God *only* wants fun, or the storms wouldn't come at all. There must be something else going on.

When we think about God, I think we make one of two mistakes: we either see Him as a Santa Claus, the deity who wants to give us everything we want, regardless of the consequences; or as a Scrooge, the God who says suffering is good for the soul, so let's pile it on. Neither reflects the God who says, "I have come that they may have life, and have it to the full" (John 10:10). God wants to give us a full, or abundant, life! He's not offering either a carefree life or a miserable life; He's offering abundant life! But the way we define abundant life and the way God defines it can diverge widely.

What Does Abundance Look Like?

In his letter, James tells us that we should "consider it pure joy, my brothers, whenever you face trials of many kinds, because you know that the testing of your faith develops perseverance" (1:2–3). Usually when a storm comes, our natural inclination is not to consider it an occasion for joy. We want the storm to go away. Yet what James is pointing to, I think, is that there is something deeper in life than the fleeting happiness that comes from our own security, something we miss when we don't have storms. Storms, I believe, are not the sum total of the abundant life, as much as they are the soil, fertilizer, and roots of the abundant life. They allow new perspectives, dreams, and attitudes to be born, attitudes that will help us soar.

Christian saints have long tasted the abundance found in suffering, often simply called joy. Mother Teresa, for instance, lived among the poorest of the poor and endured hardship, persecution, derision, and hunger. Was she happy? I think she would probably answer yes, but at the same time tell you that this is the wrong question. When we make God the focus of our lives, we find there is something deeper than happiness.

What is it that's deeper? Coming heart-to-heart with God certainly is. Blaise Pascal once said that there is a God-shaped hole in each of us that only He can fill. When we come close to Him, that filling starts. Ironically, we often begin that process of growing closer to God when we lose all else to cling to. I find it difficult, though tremendously inspiring, to read the stories of those who are suffering for their faith today. In many cases, it would be easy for them to avoid their persecution—just denounce Jesus and obey the authorities. Yet modern-day saints stand firm, regardless of opposition. To the authorities' frequent consternation, they don't lose heart. On the contrary, many finally find true joy.

A few months before the Congolese coup when Helen Roseveare was taken captive, her mission supervisor assigned her to read Foxe's *Book of Martyrs*. She wasn't thrilled about the prospect. She felt she could never be a martyr, and the book made for depressing reading. But just a few months later, she found herself praying to be martyred. Believing they were about to be killed, this group of female missionaries began to sing and praise God and were excited that at any minute they would be before Jesus. When the guns didn't fire, they almost felt angry. They had been denied the chance to see their Savior! Happiness had lost its hold on Helen, and something greater had taken its place: the ability to see beyond the things we think we want here to something that can never be snatched away.

As we grow closer to God through suffering, joy becomes more likely. You know that the joy of the Lord, and not the fleeting happiness of this world, is your strength. And when you learn that lesson, circumstances lose their ability to steal your joy. Abundance is possible because we're not confined by what we have. The sky's the limit!

Perhaps, then, when Jesus said He wanted us to live abundantly, it was not that He wanted us to have everything as much as it was that He wanted us to need God. When circumstances lose the ability to drag us down, we can live abundantly. It is not, then, that God doesn't value happiness as much as it is that God wishes for us far more.

The True Point of Life

To live in joy is to understand that *circumstances* are not the final goal; *character* is what we are working toward. We don't need easy lives; we need to remain faithful through any trial, including those excruciating ones involving loved ones. I know that's a hard thing to accept. It was certainly difficult for me, especially as a parent, and my fears affected my whole attitude toward my children. A few years ago, after losing Christopher, I started to notice that my prayers for my other children were far more concerned with what I wanted to save them *from* than with whom I wanted them to *become*. Hearing Cassie Bernall's story from the Columbine tragedy was a watershed experience for me. With a gun pointed at her, this young teenager answered yes to the question, "Do you believe in God?" She stood up for Jesus, a declaration that cost her her life. When I thought about that scenario, to my horror I realized that I would want my daughters, Katie and Rebecca, to do the same. There are things I want beyond safety. Our shopping list of things that will make us happy is actually insufficient for a truly joyful life. If we're to soar, we can't be tied down. When we put our faith in happiness, we tie ourselves to this earth and lessen our chances for joy.

Nevertheless, it's hard to give up these dreams, the anchors that hold us to the life we have built. We invest so much in those we love; should we pretend they don't matter? The apostle Paul understood this dilemma, as we see in his prayer for the Ephesian church. Among other things, he asked God that their hearts be opened so that they would know "the riches of his glorious inheritance" (1:18). *Riches* probably wasn't the first word that came to mind when the Ephesians thought of their situation. They were surrounded by people who thought persecuting them was a recipe for a good time!

But Paul knew that if the believers could only take their eyes off the things they wanted—namely security—and focus on the wonderful things God already had for them, they would not only be able to persevere, but also to live in hope and joy. He knew that the richness of life is found not in clinging to false security, but in clinging to the ultimate "Just wait!" Just wait and see what God will do. When we come to the place where we can put our lives in His hands, knowing that He offers the most abundant life we could want, then perhaps some of our wailing about storms will be stilled as we live in anticipation of what He will do.

4

God Whispers: "Am I Enough?"

What did I do to deserve this? Why would God bring such suffering? Doesn't God want me to be happy? These are some of the questions we wail during a storm. The prophet Elijah, in the story found in 1 Kings 19, also went through such a period of accusing God. He had just been the instrument for one of God's greatest acts of power, when God showed all of Israel that He was the Lord by sending fire from heaven. Yet just after this tremendous miracle, Elijah learned that Jezebel wanted to kill him and he fled into the desert and prayed to die.

Why would God snatch away his victory like that? Just as we do during storms, Elijah felt discouraged and defeated, and he took it up with God. Yet look at how God responded to the prophet. First, He sent an angel to provide Elijah with food and water. Then, when Elijah finally arrived at the holy mountain to meet with God, God didn't yell at him for his accusations. Instead, He asked Elijah why he had come—though He knew full well—giving Elijah the chance to air his grievances. Elijah replied that he had been "very zealous for the LORD God Almighty," but the people had rejected God despite His work, and now he was "the only one left" (v. 10). What was the point in continuing?

At this point in the story something really interesting happens. Elijah had just seen God's jealousy and anger and power vividly through the fire that burned up his sacrifice. But now God, as He looked at His servant in turmoil, showed a very different side of Himself. God hid Elijah in a cleft of a rock, and showed him that He was not in the wind, the earthquake, or the fire, but instead in a gentle whisper that restores the soul. When we are most desperate, God often woos us back in whispers. And I think there are some common threads to what God whispers during these times.

Though Christopher's death was the worst storm I have endured, it did not touch my sense of self-worth or my identity the way other storms have. With my son, as devastated as I was, I knew I was loved. I knew I had been a great mom to him. I knew who I was and I knew my future was secure. That was not always the case.

Five years earlier, I had faced a storm that first showed me that God can speak in whispers. After a string of painful romantic break-ups, I had finally met the man I wanted to spend the rest of my life with. He was perfect for me, I thought, and I felt so comfortable with him. But just like some cheap B movie with a clichèd plot, the day after the wedding invitations arrived he called off the wedding and our relationship. He would rather live without me.

I sank into despair. What made it worse was that rejection had been a frequent, unwelcome guest in my life. Today, I sometimes watch my girls and marvel at their enthusiasm for life and confidence in who they are. Aside from their brother's death, they have lived a life in which the sun has smiled on them. How different they are from the shy little girl I was, desperate for people to approve of me! My father walked out on us when I was two, and my stepfather followed suit a decade later. I felt like I just wasn't important enough, and though I loved God and wanted to serve Him, in the words of U2, I still hadn't found what I was looking for. I still needed other people to love me.

So during the summer after that fateful breakup, I spent several weeks challenging God, yelling at Him and demanding that He make this right. Eventually, though, like Elijah, we run out of things to say. We're exhausted and defeated. We've wailed all our questions and accusations, and we have nothing left. It is then that God often ministers. He lets us run off all the anger and bitterness, and then He bends down, embraces us, and whispers.

One summer day, when I couldn't see the sun through my tears, I went for a walk with God. I was completely drained. There was nothing else to yell. And then I heard a voice inside my head saying, "Sheila, I gave My life for you. Do you trust Me with yours? Even if he never comes back, am I enough for you?"

"Am I enough?" That is the question through storms that is often being breathed into us. Do you trust Me? Can you wait on Me? These are important questions too. But in the end, most storms boil down to that one essential point: Is God enough?

So often we're looking for a storm to end so that everything can get back to what it was, to what we feel it should be. That's the type of resolution we want. But God's healing doesn't look like that. When we know God, we are restored. God doesn't heal as much as He *is* the healing. I think that's why Paul said, "I consider everything a loss compared to the surpassing greatness of knowing Christ Jesus my Lord" (Phil. 3:8). When our hearts are increasingly joined with His, our deepest needs are met.

Saying that God is enough can feel very scary. If we admit He's enough, does that mean we're saying good-bye to the person or thing that is so vital to us? When Pat Telfer's husband, Jim, was lying in the hospital after being diagnosed with congestive heart failure, Pat knew the end could very easily be near. She was driving down the highway, heading to visit her husband, when God asked her, "Can you let go and just trust me?" Saying yes to God felt like saying good-bye to Jim. With tears streaming down her face, she had to physically hold up an open hand to God, symbolizing that she was giving Jim to Him. Though it was agonizing, she had to proclaim that God would be enough. She knew that if she didn't, a part of her would always be invested in circumstances here on earth, and her joy could be taken away.

To declare that God is enough certainly feels like we're saying good-bye, perhaps before we even need to. It's a wrenching experience. It's admitting that your marriage may not be restored, that your husband may not be healed, or that you may never walk again. But something happens when we are able to say that God is enough. We are free to do the real work that comes with walking through these storms.

The morning of Christopher's surgery, I arrived at the hospital at 6:00. They would be taking him in at 7:30, and I knew I might never see him again. I wanted some time with him. As I cradled him in my arms—his tiny body attached to many monitors—I looked into his pinched face, so small from all the weight he had lost during his ordeal. And I said good-bye. "Mommy's going to be fine," I said to him. "It's all right if you have to go. I love you so much, and I don't want you to be in pain. So whether you're with Jesus or with me, I will love you. Good-bye, my baby." I am so grateful to have had that time to say good-bye to him in peace. I knew God was enough, and so I could let Christopher go.

Diane Komp is a pediatric oncologist—a kids' cancer doctor—who came to faith after watching God work in the lives of her little patients and their families. One particular incident that opened her eyes to God happened one night with a little seven-year-old girl who had been battling leukemia almost her whole life. Her family was gathered around her bedside because they knew her time was short. They were praying, holding her hands, and saying good-bye. And then, all of a sudden, the little girl sat up, her face radiant, and said, "Oh, Mommy, can you hear the angels? The singing! I've never heard such beautiful singing!" With that, she lay down and was gone.

There was not a dry eye in that hospital room, including Dr. Komp's. But that family, because they were able to say that God is enough, were able to look through the storm to what lay beyond. When they were sitting around her bed, they weren't in agony. They were at peace, even if that peace was tinged with sadness, and so they could send their daughter to Jesus. And God gave them a blessing in return. God opened up a window to heaven, as Dr. Komp calls it, and allowed the little girl and her family to get a glimpse of heaven together and share that joy.

To say God is enough is to let go of those things you're desperately trying to keep. It doesn't mean that those people or things will not be given back to you. It does mean that you are setting them free, to find resolution in peace. That summer when my fiancé left me, I struggled with God's question, "Am I enough?" over and over again, until finally I resolved that no matter what happened, I would be with God. Nobody could ever fill my heart the way God could. And I would not abandon Him, even if my dreams for this life did not come true.

As a mom, my dreams did not come true. My son did die. In that earlier summer, however, things turned out quite differently. Keith came back into my life a few months later, and we were married soon afterward. I cannot imagine my life without him. We have walked through so much together and have grown stronger. Today we speak at marriage conferences, encouraging others to develop the oneness that God designed for marriage and that we are striving for. And yet, as wonderful as our marriage is, I know it is not what my life is built on. I love my husband dearly, but I also know that God is enough.

Being able to say that is a healing experience. It sets us free from the compulsion to meet our needs here on earth with things that are fleeting, that we cannot control. To know that God is enough, no matter what may come, frees us from fear. As 2 Corinthians 4:18 says, "We fix our eyes not on what is seen, but on what is unseen. For what is seen is temporary, but what is unseen is eternal."

Not all of us are ready to lay all at the foot of the cross. I met Maureen at a speaking engagement for young moms. She had tagged along with her daughter and grandchildren, who had consumed her life ever since her husband had walked out four years earlier. He had rejected her, rejected the faith, and moved in with another woman.

Maureen threw herself into Scripture, but what she was searching for was a guarantee that she could hold onto, a promise that said her husband would come back. She found a number of verses that seemed to offer such an assurance, so she claimed them, wrote them down, and carried them in her wallet. I asked her, gently, what would happen if her husband never returned? She wouldn't even consider such a scenario. He would return, she told me.

I pray that he will, but I also know many women, including my own mother, who were not so blessed. Unfortunately, in this life we must often carry the consequences for others' sin. And as long as Maureen bases her future on her husband's return, she will not be able to move on. In Philippians 3:13, Paul tells the people to forget what is behind and strain toward what is ahead. Don't look to the past for your fulfillment; look to what God will do. Does this mean Maureen should give up waiting for him to come back? I can't say, for I believe God speaks to each of us individually. But if she can let go of her fears enough to sit and listen to God's whisper, I believe she will hear God saying, "Am I enough?" Knowing that God is enough will set her free to live life with joy, whether or not her husband returns.

Sometimes those of us who walk with God build our lives around more than just Him. These things are often very good: our families, our ministries, our callings. Yet as worthwhile as they are, they should never take God's place. If we dare to walk out into the desert and have it out with God, I believe we too will eventually hear Him whisper, "Am I enough?" Don't be alarmed if you can't answer right away. Don't worry if this is a hard, wrenching question. But don't run from it, either. Carry it with you. Embrace it. For when we can let Jesus speak those words to our souls, we can begin the process of truly living a life anchored in Him.

5

God Whispers: "Do You Remember That You Are Dust?"

"Am I enough?" is the starting point, the big question God asks that helps us to clarify how we are going to weather a storm. It is not, however, the only question God whispers. As the winds rage and the rain beats down during my storms, I often hear God ask a far gentler question, "Do you remember that you are dust?"

Perhaps it is because I like to wax poetic that I hear it phrased that way. God may ask you the same thing in another way: "Are you demanding too much of yourself? Can you give yourself a break? Do you remember that you are only human?" During storms, sometimes all we can do is duck, huddle under the umbrella, and wait it out. And that is okay.

The secretary at my church, Becky Rodberg, lost her son Craig in an automobile accident three years ago. He was 29, married, the father of a girl about to turn three, and he and his wife had a baby on the way. The grief was devastating. There were days when the only sound in her head were these words, recited over and over: "Left foot, right foot, inhale, exhale. Repeat action." It was all she could do to get through the next five minutes, let alone cope, recover, minister to others, or work through any of her feelings. Sometimes storms bowl us over and we feel powerless, wondering how we can even take that next breath.

Allowing for Grief

Unfortunately, we don't always give ourselves the permission to walk through those valleys when living is all we can do. We try to deny our feelings, or we berate ourselves for how intense they are. We may even play the role of our own personal inquisitor, demanding of ourselves: Why can't you get over this? Why can't you keep it all together? Instead of hearing God's whispers, we hear our own "shoulds," and some of the most fervent "shoulds" we utter relate to grief. You *should* be able to handle this. You *should* be able to get through this. You *should* be a lot stronger than you are.

I think we say these "shoulds" because we want to emerge on the other side of these strong, suffocating feelings of loss. If we can just pull it together, maybe we can stop hurting. Is this the way humans are supposed to work, though? Is this how we "should" work? Remember that the reason we hurt is because we also love. God created us with a deep need for connection, and when we love, we will experience joy and intense satisfaction. When death separates, we often experience the depth of that connection in a new way. It's a painful revelation, but one that can be more sweet than bitter, for having had that love, even if the object of it is snatched from you, changes your heart. Many who have faced this abyss report that they can now feel more deeply, love more richly, and live more profoundly. They know how valuable love is. Grieving, then, is almost like a romantic courtship in reverse. You experience this flood of love feelings, but the object of your love is gone. The solution is not to get rid of the love, to paper over it so that it doesn't matter anymore, or to deny it because it's too painful. The solution, instead, is to know that in feeling that love, you celebrate that life.

Psychologist Scott Peck has said that the cause of most psychological struggle is pain avoidance. When we love someone or something dearly, it's clear we can't avoid pain when that person or thing is taken away. But in our desperation to feel better, we may try to smother these grief feelings because we don't want to touch them. They're too deep. Don't be afraid to touch them. It's part of being human, and to deny them is, as Peck says, to inadvertently cause more harm.

God, who made us this way, is intimately aware of our sorrow. I think we forget this, believing instead that when God heals, we will feel perfect again, as if God views us as flawed when we are sad. We mistakenly fear that if we're sad, it must mean that we can't accept His healing, or even that we're rejecting Him altogether. If this were true, I doubt that the Bible would speak with such tenderness about tears. At one point, God tells us that our tears are so precious that He has bottled them up (Ps. 56:8 NRSV). We will have tears on this earth, and these tears matter to God. He takes them on Himself. He carries our sorrows on the cross. And then He makes this promise: in the new heaven and the new earth, there will be no more tears (Rev. 21:4). On this side of heaven we will cry and we will mourn. Don't expect that your crying or mourning should disappear, or that tears are symptoms of weakness or a lack of faith. You are simply being human, which is, after all, what you were created to be.

One day, I trust, you will be able to remember with laughter, and not only with tears. Embrace that day when it comes, but don't rush it. Let your heart lead you, for God says that weeping and mourning are valid, vital, and legitimate parts of the human experience. While you are in the valley, they will be your companions. And that is all right.

Allowing for Healing

Unfortunately, when the tears finally stop, we sometimes hear other "shoulds": You shouldn't be so happy, so normal, so alive. If you're happy now, then you didn't really love enough.

The death of a child is one of the most difficult losses to accept, since it feels as if the physical laws of the universe have been violated.

You needed that child far more than you need the very air you breathe, and yet that child is gone, and your lungs keep working. When a child dies, especially a baby who did not have the chance to become part of your daily routine, on the outside it is almost as if he or she never existed. And yet, that child was your very heart. If you let go of your grief, it is as if you are letting go of the only thing that still ties you to your baby. So you cling to that grief, and if a day comes when the grief doesn't rear its head, you accuse yourself of forgetting.

I think we misunderstand how grief works. It isn't something that disappears in time. When my husband was in medical school, they taught him a way to think of grief that helped us through Christopher's death. Many people picture the course of grief as if it's a straight line on a graph, diminishing with time until it disappears. In other words, there will be a day when it won't hurt at all.

The human heart doesn't work this way. Instead, grief looks a lot more like a bar graph. Early in the grieving process, the bars are thick and tall, lasting a long time. As time passes, the bars get further apart. There may be hours, days, weeks, or months when you don't feel badly. You function normally. But then all of a sudden it will hit you—on an anniversary, or when you hear a song on the radio or see a picture—and you will be plunged back into that sea of raw emotion. As time passes, such episodes will usually not last as long, though they will still occur. We are never over grief. It becomes part of us, like a shawl we wrap around our shoulders. But it does not always consume us.

So embrace those moments when you feel peace, because there will be moments—even if it's days, weeks, or years later—when the grief will return, unbidden, in full force. Be grateful for good days and do not feel guilty for them. Smiling is not betraying your child, or your husband, or your wife. Moving on, having another child, marrying again, or even just laughing at a joke, is not negating any love you had for someone. Though we must tread carefully when we rebuild our lives after losses, the rebuilding itself is not a bad thing. God whispers to us: Remember that you are human. Remember that separation will hurt and wound deeply. But remember, too, that you were made to survive. Do not feel guilty if you do.

Allowing for Our Physical Limits

Dealing with emotions in storms is difficult enough, but sometimes the actual circumstances of a storm make it even harder to cope with life. When I was speaking at a women's coffee hour, I met Belinda, a gracious woman who was desperate to find some time to rejuvenate with God. Her family had faced tremendous tragedy over the previous two years. First, her son-in-law had abandoned her daughter, leaving the devastated woman with two young children to care for and the necessity of finding a job. Just a year later, Belinda's daughter-in-law died tragically, less than three months after giving birth to her second child. Now four young children desperately needed this grandma's love and care while their remaining parents picked up the pieces of their lives. At the same time, Belinda's mother was ill. What was she to do? How could she ever get enough rest and time to herself to keep going?

She could not do it all, nor should she. She needed to distinguish between what was in her power to do well and what was not. God whispers: Remember, my beloved, that you are only dust. There was only so much of her to go around.

All of us have times in our lives when we cannot handle alone everything that is on our plate. God even made allowances for these times. In Galatians 6:2, He instructs us to "carry each other's burdens, and in this way you will fulfill the law of Christ." We are stronger together. Yet, because it seems an admission that we can't cope, it can be hard to ask for help. My friend Susan was once going through a terrible week. As a child, she had endured fourth-degree burns on her legs, and had to have massive surgery over a period of decades to help her. Now, as an adult, she had a recurrence of the frequent infections that had plagued her in childhood, and she had to stay off her feet for a time. But she had two small children at home who needed care. Her friends rallied around her, taking shifts at her house to watch the kids and do the housework so she wouldn't need to stand. Yet Susan had a hard time accepting the help. "I just feel badly that people had to give up their week to help me!" she said sheepishly as she rose from her chair yet again to get the children something. Despite our protests, she wouldn't stay put. She didn't realize how privileged we felt that we could be of help.

Sometimes we need to see a situation through God's eyes. God blesses people when they serve others. When we let others help, we actually bless them! So often when a friend is going through a loss, illness, or another crisis, people are desperate to help but they don't know what to do or to say. Should I stay away? Should I phone? When Christopher died, after receiving my sixth bouquet of flowers, I let it be known that chocolates were helpful too, as were meals, and soon our kitchen was overflowing. People's hearts were breaking for us, and they wanted to do something that would help. They just needed to be given the word.

God often uses others to carry us through storms, but too often their human frailty makes us discount them. People say incredibly stupid things in their desire to say something—anything—profound. I had people say to me, on the death of my son, "At least you know you can have children," or "It was obviously meant to be this way," or "He's so much better off now." Perhaps these things were all true, but they were also hurtful and completely unnecessary to voice. Sometimes when we walk through storms, we react to these sorts of comments with such hurt and anger that we shut others out. Let's not seal ourselves off when we face difficult times. We need others, and God placed us in a body of believers for a reason. Though that body is fallible, if we give people a chance, we open everybody up to blessing.

Allowing for Our Failures

Accepting our emotions and physical limitations through storms is hard, but it is perhaps more difficult to accept what we see as our failures, especially when it seems our whole identity is at stake. In our mission-statement world, it is hard to see through the clouds when the purpose of our lives seems gone, or the defining element of who we are has been swept from us. So when God whispers, "Remember, you are dust," I think He's also saying, "Remember, your plans will come to dust." So often we judge our lives on this earth in terms of effectiveness, as if we are all giant corporations trying to achieve a greater market share for God. Because of this, setbacks hit us especially hard.

Yet God does not see effectiveness as we do. If we need to take some years off to study, to pray, to seek God's will, or even to deal with past hurts or ministry and job disruption, God does not necessarily view this as failure. He, after all, created our complex personalities with all their needs. If you spend a few years in limbo, He does not think your life is wasted. Jesus spent time in the wilderness; so did Abraham, Elijah, John the Baptist, the nation of Israel, and many beloved prophets of God. The wilderness does not necessarily represent wasted days or months or years. It can be a time of great refining, when we become the kind of person God is molding us to be. He judges not only by what we accomplish but also, and even more importantly, by where our hearts are. If we aren't productive for a time but are being molded as clay by the potter, God is pleased with that.

The prophet Jeremiah struggled with despondency and apparent failure his whole life. In his ministry he was derided and ridiculed and won few followers. Yet today, more than 2,500 years after his death, whenever we sing "Great is Thy Faithfulness," or quote "'for I know the plans I have for you,' says the LORD," or think of the heart of stone becoming the heart of flesh, we do so because Jeremiah was faithful even when it looked on the outside like he was completely ineffective. He couldn't see the big picture, but God used him because of his willingness. He didn't handle the storms perfectly, but in the end it was his obedience, not his success, that made him a hero of the faith.

Today God still whispers to us, "Remember that you are dust, but I am God. Don't try to be Me. Don't think you need all the answers, all the strength, all the trophies. You don't need success to win My approval. You just need Me." So let's not despise wilderness days, when disappointment hits as the plans of our lives lie scattered at our feet. God does not despise those days, and as we walk through that desert sand, it is often easier to see His footprints.

6

God Whispers: "Can I Carry You?"

Ever since the Garden of Eden, God has been struggling as an unrequited lover. He yearned to rescue Israel, but over and over again the Old Testament nations of Israel and Judah rejected Him. Jesus, while looking over Jerusalem, cried out, "O Jerusalem, Jerusalem, you who kill the prophets and stone those sent to you, how often I have longed to gather your children together, as a hen gathers her chicks under her wings" (Matt. 23:37). God's heart is one that longs to comfort.

The last whispered question is the one that perhaps touches our hearts the most: "Can you let Me carry you? Can I bind up your wounds, heal your heart, embrace you?" Yet despite God's pleas, we often wall ourselves off from Him.

In the fifth chapter of his gospel, John tells the story of a man who had been crippled for thirty-eight years. Every day, this man lay by a pool with miraculous properties, but he was never able to crawl into that pool himself. When Jesus saw him, He asked, "Do you want to be healed?" What a strange question! Hadn't the man demonstrated it by remaining near the only source of help he knew? Yet instead of answering, the man proceeded to give all the reasons why healing was impossible. He was too busy concentrating on his problems. I think God asks us the same question. Do you want to be healed? But how will we answer?

We've talked about how there are times when all we can do is inhale, exhale, repeat. Touching that pain is important. But it does not always have to feel this intense. A time for healing can come. King Solomon wrote about such times in Ecclesiastes 3, when he said, "There is a time for everything, and a season for every activity under heaven: . . . a time to weep and a time to laugh, a time to mourn and a time to dance, a time to scatter stones and a time to gather them" (vv. 1, 4–5). When the stones of our lives are scattered, it seems hard to imagine a time when we may gather them again. When we mourn, how can we turn to dancing? We can't, I don't think, unless God carries us to that point.

Most of us yearn to be free from hurt, but we find healing difficult to accept. We stare at the scattered stones, and we're afraid to gather them and build again because it may not be the same, and it may not be as good. The scattered stones are all that remains of the life we lived and loved, needed and breathed. How can we move beyond the rubble?

Letting God Minister

David experienced this struggle many times in his life. Listen to his heart in Psalm 40:

> I waited patiently for the Lord;
>   he turned to me and heard my cry.
> He lifted me out of the slimy pit,
>   out of the mud and mire;
> he set my feet on a rock
>   and gave me a firm place to stand.
> He put a new song in my mouth,
>   a hymn of praise to our God.
> Many will see and fear
>   and put their trust in the LORD. (vv. 1–3)

David was crying out to God, and God gave him a "new song" to sing, a song of praise. Yet if you look at the remainder of that psalm, you'll see that David's circumstances did not change. People were still seeking his life (v. 14), troubles still surrounded him (v. 12), and he still dealt with guilt (v. 12). He was in dire straits. The stones were still scattered! Yet God had lifted him out of the pit that he felt he was in. He was able to praise God, to tell of God's wonderful works, even to desire to do God's will. David had a heart change, not necessarily a life change. And that is what rescued him. And once he had that heart change, he could build with the stones once again.

Many times that's exactly what we need. We cry out to God to change our circumstances, and yet our true need is for God to change our hearts. In this psalm, God did so by giving David a new song to sing, reminding David of his precious relationship with Him, a relationship that could not be taken away. In the midst of storms, this is a powerful message. When we endure a storm, we feel as if everything is out of our control. Things are swirling all around us, and we are powerless to stop it, to end the hurt, to find peace. Yet God, as He gives us these new songs, reminds us that, through Him, we are not powerless at all.

He reminds us again of what we do know, of the relationship we have with Him which has not changed. It's a reaffirmation of our personhood: no matter what happens, we can act, and we can will to respond to God. Even if our feelings aren't cooperating, we can still decide to rest in Him. He gives us that ability. We are not solely victims of the tornadoes around us. We can find shelter and avoid being blown over simply by remembering our essential identity in God. We are His, and we are never alone. We are neither confined nor defined by our circumstances.

My friend Cheryl had an experience similar to David's heart change. Her daughter Lindsay, the middle of three children, had been born with severe mental and physical handicaps, and her health had been a constant struggle. After a particularly horrendous week when everything seemed to have gone wrong, Cheryl found herself driving Lindsay down the highway, heading for yet another hospital admission. She didn't know how she could cope. So Cheryl, a praise leader at her church, prayed, "God, just give me a song. I need a song to carry me through." And on that highway, she received these words:

> I believe that your promises are true.
> I believe what you say you will do.
> Even though I cannot see your ways,
> I know you're there for me and
> I believe that your promises are true.
> You've promised life to me, you've promised peace,
> you said you would not leave me and will not forsake me,
> you promised joy with the morning sun,
> and strength through the night,
> and I believe that your promises are true.

"As I was singing those words in the car, and in the hospital over the next few days, I didn't feel any of them," Cheryl says. "I felt so low, so abandoned, so discouraged. But those words gave me something to keep saying, to keep encouraging myself in the Lord. And as I said them, they did become true." What a gift from God.

God has a habit of reminding people that His strength is made perfect in weakness. Becky, the woman in the last chapter who lost her son, vividly was shown this truth years before, through a different loss. Abandoned, betrayed, and rejected by her husband, this newly divorced woman was reeling. Yet through it all she was trying to be an example to her adult children as to how a Christian can get through a separation and divorce and still maintain her faith. She was also coping with the chaos of holding down multiple part-time jobs to support herself. Life was exhausting. Sunday morning church services, for her, were the chance to grieve all she had lost, and it had been that way for some time. One Sunday, though, as she poured out her heart to God during the prayer time, she felt Him saying, "Becky, everyone has seen your pain. Now it's time for them to see what I can do for you." And finally she let Him. Jesus wants to change us so that we are not simply defined by our difficulties. That man by the pool, though he thought he wanted healing, could not see himself as separate from his problems. They constituted his identity. But that's not the way Jesus sees us. Our pasts may still affect us; we may still bear scars, but they are no longer open wounds. When we let God carry us, we begin the healing process.

Often in Scripture, after God had an intense encounter with someone, He changed that person's name. Simon became Peter, the rock on whom God would build His church, when he professed that Jesus was the Son of God. Abram, "exalted father," became Abraham, "father of many," after God made a covenant with him to make him into a mighty nation. Their new names reflected what God would do, not where they had come from. But this naming act is not confined to the giants in Scripture. In Revelation 2:17, God gives new names that only we know to those of us who overcome. God names us in a personal, intimate way often borne out of our victory over difficulties, the very painful process when God first became our sustainer, our ultimate rock.

I think God uses this strategy because when our names change, the way we think of ourselves changes. Instead of being abuse victims, we become children of God. Instead of being mistakes, we become cherished of God. Instead of being the abandoned wife, we become brides of the Beloved. Just think, God knows your new name, and He has engraved you on the palms of His hands (Isa. 49:16).

As you struggle through this storm, can you let God carry you? When you place yourself in His hands, you start the process of becoming a new person with a new name. How will God name you? How will He carry you through this storm? Don't be afraid to ask. He is there, waiting to shelter you, cradle you, and carry you through to the other side.

7

God Whispers: "This Life Is Not All There Is"

Adorning our family room walls are pictures from various adventures we have taken together: hiking the Grand Canyon, visiting an iguana farm in Belize, standing in awe of the Alaskan glaciers. But my favorite picture features my husband front and center, with our then five-year-old daughter on his shoulders, and Salisbury Cathedral towering in the background.

Salisbury Cathedral is majestic, and perhaps all the more so because it was built in the thirteenth century. Topped with the tallest church spire in England, it was first erected when most people still lived in tiny hovels.

It's easy to think that the church should have spent that money on the people rather than putting it into a building, but I'm not so certain the church leaders chose wrongly. During the Middle Ages, people lived brutal, short lives. Malnourishment was rampant. The Plague ravaged Europe. Simple infection could steal a person's limb or a person's life. What did the populace really need? Perhaps an assurance that there was something beyond this life—something majestic, something beautiful, and something bigger than they could even imagine.

While touring through those old churches, one gets the sense of the majesty of God. Those buildings were partly erected as a promise, an outstretched offer of hope to the people. Walk into the ornate structures and you can almost hear the walls whisper: *There is something beyond. This is not all there is.*

Too often today, people think of heaven as a crutch, that those who talk about heaven do so only because they can't bear their lives. We're supposed to find joy and peace now, not just wait for heaven! To a certain extent, that's true. But perhaps the pendulum has swung too far from the hope of heaven, so that we tend to think of our earthly lives as being the sum total of our existence. We may pay lip service to heaven when we sing that verse of Amazing Grace—"When we've been there ten thousand years..."—but if you were to ask most people what they were looking forward to, heaven is not the first thing they'd name. We yearn for marriage, for children, for retirement, for graduation, for vacation. We're looking forward to what we can taste here, not what we can taste there.

The End of the Beginning Is Coming

And so, I believe, the final thing God whispers to us in our pain is His promise: "This is not all there is. There is something more!"

The early Christians understood this. Do you remember how excited Paul was about heaven? He said in Philippians, which he wrote while he was chained in prison, "For to me, living is Christ and dying is gain" (1:21, NRSV). Hoping for heaven is not saying, "Well, at least when I die I'll still go on." Rather, it's "Something even better is waiting for me! I've only just begun to live!"

Winston Churchill articulated something similar during one of his rousing speeches in World War II. Today, with hindsight, we know the war ended in decisive victory for the Allies, but in 1940 and 1941 that victory was still far off—and rather doubtful. The United Kingdom stood alone in Western Europe against the Nazis. Belgium had fallen.

France had fallen. The Netherlands had fallen. Britain had lost its territories in the Far East. And the Allies had to be hastily evacuated at Dunkirk.

And then, finally, on November 10, 1942, Britain had something to celebrate. Montgomery had managed to push Rommel's forces back in Egypt, winning in North Africa.

Winston Churchill rallied his people with these words: "This is not the end. It is not even the beginning of the end. But it is, perhaps, the end of the beginning." The turning point had come.

Have you been walking through the fog of war in your own life, where circumstances look bleak? You've suffered defeat after defeat. And yet, in that darkness, I believe God is whispering, "This is not the end. It is not even the beginning of the end. But it is, perhaps, the end of the beginning."

This life on earth is your beginning—it's only a blink of an eye in comparison to eternity. We think of this as our real life, and yet this life, on average, will last eight and a half decades. That life will last forever.

One day recently, when I was feeling lonely, the thought occurred to me that the best friend I will ever have I probably have not met yet. She may be a lovely saint of a woman who died a millennium ago in France, but her mansion will be right next to mine, and oh, we will have fun! In this life, if I only have eighty-odd years, I'm going to spend them knitting. I adore knitting, and if time is short I am not going to spend it trying to master a different craft. But in the next life, when time is no object, I am going to learn to quilt. I'll mix fabrics together to create a stunning mosaic that will praise God in a whole new way. It really will be glorious.

Heaven Has a Throne

Beyond these thoughts that make me giggle, though, is something even better: the certainty, soothing and exciting at the same time, that one day I will see Jesus. Like Paul wrote in 1 Corinthians 13:12: "For now we see in a mirror, dimly, but then we will see face to face. Now

I know only in part; then I will know fully, even as I have been fully known" (NRSV). To be fully known, to see face to face—that is the promise not just of reconciliation with God, but of true and utter and glorious intimacy. That deep longing in our souls will finally be met.

Many people hope for heaven, where they'll see all their relatives and friends who have passed on, and live an easy life forever. These hopes are natural. But they are also empty and meaningless if we don't first hope for the Person who inhabits heaven, and to whom all of heaven gravitates. Heaven without Christ is a fairytale. Heaven with Christ is a homecoming party when all our hopes will be realized. And it is only through Christ that heaven is even possible. As He said, "I am the way, and the truth, and the life. No one comes to the Father except through me" (John 14:6).

When Jesus died, He did so with the primary purpose that we could have intimacy with God. The ugliness, the sin inside us that kept us from God, was all heaped on Him. And now we also have the Holy Spirit living in us, so that we are never, ever alone. And our hearts rejoice.

Today we are completely reconciled. We are completely heirs. We are completely adopted into God's family. And yet there is still some distance, because we can't physically see Him. One day that distance, that fog, will be wiped away. That's something to look forward to!

If we had Paul's attitude that to die is gain, perhaps we would find the disappointments, hardships, and even soul-crushing heartaches of this life easier to navigate. We would have more of an eternal perspective, because we would be focused first and foremost on that reunion.

Listen to what Paul says in Philippians 3:12–14:

> Not that I have already obtained this or have already reached the goal; but I press on to make it my own, because Christ Jesus has made me his own. Beloved, I do not consider that I have made it my own; but this one thing I do: forgetting what lies behind and straining forward to what lies ahead, I press on toward the goal for the prize of the heavenly call of God in Christ Jesus. (NRSV)

The goal of Paul's life is not happiness or success here on earth; it is the heavenly call of God in Christ. Even in this life, our focus is to be heavenward.

One of the greatest mistakes we can make, then, is to try to turn this earth into our heaven. Yes, all creation groans for Christ's return, when He will put all things right. Yes, part of our role is to work to restore broken relationships and this broken earth. Yes, God's heart is consumed with His people here, and He wants us to be His hands and feet to minister to those around us. This life does matter dearly, and God knows we are dust, and He cares about us here. But nevertheless, we should never mistake this earth for the one that is to come, or this life for the one that is promised.

Let's Not Mistake This Earth for Heaven

However, it is all too easy to do that, because our lives present the possibility of ease and abundance. Think about this: if you live in North America or Western Europe, you are likely richer than Henry VIII was. He was the richest man of his time—king of England in the 1500s—yet he did not have Advil. He didn't have anesthetic, either, and personally I'm a big fan of anesthetic. He didn't have central heating, or indoor plumbing, or refrigeration. In fact, despite Henry's love of fashion, it's quite likely that everyone reading this owns more clothes than he did.

We live in a time of abundance, and I wonder if we realize how very strange historically this is. The poor in North America today are more likely to suffer from obesity than from hunger. Very few people will suffer the death of a child, though at one time this was so commonplace that people didn't even give their children names for the first few weeks of life in case disease stole them. When my husband and I spent a summer tracing our family tree, we found many families with three children named "John." The first John would die, so the next one would inherit the name. Many parents steeled themselves against becoming too attached to infants, because death was all too common.

During that summer of genealogy, we also visited an old family graveyard in rural Quebec, and there, on one gravestone, was listed the names of four children, all under the age of six, and all having died within one week during a cholera epidemic. The family went on to have ten more children, but at the time, those four were all those parents had.

As horrible as that was, other gravestones told the same heartbreaking story. Early death was not uncommon. Today, because lives are so rarely cut short, when it does happen we are caught off-guard. Death has always been a tragedy, but now it's accompanied by an even greater feeling of injustice. Death shouldn't happen, not with modern medicine, not with our hospitals, not with our drugs. Our advances make the tragedy that much harder to accept.

These same advances also encourage us to put more of our focus on this earth. If tragedy is remote, we are freer to cling to the blessings we've been given. We build our lives around the people we love and cherish, and the tangible things we have, and understandably so. We are to love deeply, and extravagantly, and wholeheartedly. Yet in that loving, if we are not careful, we can rob ourselves of real joy.

When my oldest daughter Rebecca was three, she thought sharing was an extremely silly idea invented by grown-ups. Twice a week, when we would venture to the neighborhood playgroup, she would make a beeline to the little plastic grocery cart that was part of the kitchen play set. She would wheel that grocery cart around all of the toy boxes, flinging anything she enjoyed inside. Then she would steer that grocery cart to the corner and hurl her little body on top, preventing any other child from touching the toys she deemed hers.

I used to watch in amusement, waiting for it to dawn on her that the whole time she was preventing other children from playing with these favorite items, she wasn't playing with them either. She was too busy protecting them to enjoy them.

Are you so busy protecting those you love, or even steeling yourself against the worst, that you are unable to enjoy the life you have been given? When we focus on making sure we don't lose anything, joy is often the first casualty. We fail to live that big life we truly long for.

Flashes of Joy Even During Pain

Perhaps it's easier to explain this if we go back to first principles and try to understand that little word: "joy." C.S. Lewis, in his autobiography *Surprised by Joy*, tries to define that nebulous word. After much reflection, he summarized joy, which he described as "flashes" of intense exaltation, like this:

> I call it Joy, which is here a technical term and must be sharply distinguished both from Happiness and Pleasure. Joy (in my sense) has indeed one characteristic, and one only, in common with them; the fact that anyone who has experienced it will want it again... I doubt whether anyone who has tasted it would ever, if both were in his power, exchange it for all the pleasures in the world.[1]

What is the essential difference between joy and happiness? Joy, in Lewis' mind, does not depend on circumstances, as happiness does. Instead, joy is like a moment when God lifts back the veil that separates us from Him and lets us feel that flash of divine intimacy—that flash of heaven.

Interestingly, Lewis goes on to conclude that joy actually has more in common with grief than it does with happiness. Happiness is shallow; in grief, on the other hand, we often feel deep intimacy with God. We share that longing for reconciliation and relationship. We feel that flash of heaven.

I remember a moment of true joy. Just like Lewis described, it was like a burst of sunlight on an overcast day. I was walking to the hospital in August of 1996, when Christopher lay in the NICU, and I remember thinking to myself, "I don't know what will happen tomorrow, or next week, or next year. I don't know what will happen after Christopher's surgery. But what I do know is that today I have

---

[1] C.S. Lewis. *Surprised by Joy* (London, UK: Collins, Fount Paperback, 1987), p. 20. Original copyright 1955.

a daughter I love, a son I love, and a husband I love. My God is carrying me, even today. I am so blessed." And I decided to live that day enjoying every minute.

That joy in the moment is so much easier if we have an eternal perspective. When we define our lives by what God has given us here on this earth, our tendency is to snatch those things and hold them tightly in our clenched hands. When we know instead that this really is only the end of the beginning, and that God truly is enough, we can open our hands and enjoy our blessings so much more.

Where Is Our Home?

That's why focusing on heaven does not mean that we fail to love here on this earth. On the contrary, it means that we can live a bigger life by saying, with Paul, "For to me, living is Christ and dying is gain." We love these things dearly, but they are not the sum total of our lives. That eternal perspective gives us a bigger life.

My husband and I are World War II buffs, and one of our favorite miniseries is *Band of Brothers*, which we re-watch annually. Covering the adventures of Easy Company of the 101st Airborne, the series follows the soldiers from training through D-Day and then to heavy fighting leading to the defeat of Germany. Easy Company, always in the thick of things, suffered the highest casualty rate of the American troops in the European theatre.

One particular scene focuses on Private Albert Blythe, who froze, terrified, after parachuting into France. A few days later, the men are hunkered down in trenches, preparing to assault a fortified town. Blythe is petrified. Then a lieutenant from a neighboring company, patrolling the line, walks by and starts up a conversation. Sensing the private's fear, he says, "You know what you're problem is, Blythe? You don't realize you're already dead."

For the rest of the series, viewers witness Lieutenant Spiers doing incredibly brave things—sprinting in front of machine gun fire to warn the Brits of the whereabouts of German artillery; leading a charge over open terrain, bullets flying; running in front of his men into battle. He never flinched. And yet he survived that war relatively unscathed. He did huge, courageous things because he had this thought in his mind: "You are already dead."

If you know Christ, you are already dead, too. Your citizenship is not on this earth—it is in heaven (Philippians 3:20). Eternal life is not something we will be given one day when we leave this earth. Our eternal life has already begun. The old things have passed away, and the new have come. This is our new life, and one day we will see it come to completion and fulfillment when we climb up onto the lap of the One who gave Himself for us.

You cannot feel His arms today in the same way you will then, but that does not mean those arms don't hold you up, and that those arms will not one day carry you from this life into the next. Life is just a continuation. Maybe if we could understand that more, we could live with an open hand to God. We could live a big life.

Buddhists believe the route to the "big life" is not to focus on God but to focus on nothing. In their beliefs, to stop suffering you simply must end desire. If we didn't desire anything, we wouldn't suffer when we lost it. The goal, then, is to reach an elevated existence where the outer world does not matter. Love and desire disappear.

In focusing on our heavenly call in Christ, though, the goal is not to get rid of desire or love, or to say that this life is unimportant. Instead, it's to find that our greatest desire is not met in things here but in a Person. We are created for intimacy, and in Christ on the cross we are given the gift of having our hearts once again forged with His. And He is not a God who is indifferent to our weaknesses or feelings. He knows we are dust. He is a God who bleeds. He is a God who cries. And most of all, He is a God who rose from the dead to live within us today, so that we can feel those flashes of joy, those flashes of heaven, those flashes of true intimacy even in the deepest parts of our pain.

When I go on speaking trips, one of my favorite times to fly is when the sky is overcast and grey. The plan takes off and ascends as you gaze down at the bleak, joyless landscape. Soon you can't see anything because the grey clouds envelop the plane. But as the plane climbs higher, something marvelous happens. The plane emerges from the clouds, and the sun bursts forth! Yet the sun was shining brightly the whole time. The clouds just prevented us from seeing it.

In our pain, sometimes all we can see is the clouds. Yet one day, if we let Him, God will carry us from this life into the next. We will close our eyes on this earth and wake up beholding the face of One who loves us more than anyone else ever could. He knows we are dust; He doesn't expect us not to cry, or not to doubt, or not to hurt. He simply says, "In your hurt, look to me. Know that I am enough. Know that I am real. Hope and trust in me."

Can you do that? Can you reach out your clenched fist and open it heavenward? These clouds you see are not all there is. And as God whispers to you, "This is not all there is," peek behind the veil. Look above those clouds. A marvelous reunion is waiting for us, and it is more than we could ever ask for or imagine.

For Reflection

Chapter 1: We Cry: "What Did I Do to Deserve This?"

1. In what areas of your life do you feel guilty? Do you feel as if you don't live up to expectations? Are you haunted by your past? Write down what you feel you have done wrong, and what you feel you should have done instead. Then if any forgiveness is needed, pray and ask God to give you His mind about these things. Commit Romans 8:1 to memory, and recite it several times a day.

2. Read 1 Corinthians 10:13, and commit it to memory. Can you trust God to provide a way for you to get through your storm?

Chapter 2: We Cry: "Why Does God Let Me Suffer?"

1. How does God feel about suffering? Look at how Jesus reacted to people's deaths. Read Matthew 14:1–14 (John the Baptist) and John 11:17–44 (Lazarus).

2. How does God view calamity and grief? Read Lamentations 3:33 and Psalm 116:15 to see God's attitude toward our deepest pain. Write down these truths.

3. What comfort does God promise? Read what He says about tears in Psalm 56:8 and Revelation 21:1–4.

Chapter 3: We Cry: "Don't You Want Me to Be Happy?"

1. Read the story of Hagar in Genesis 16:1–15 and 21:8–21. This poor girl was separated from her family, sold as a slave, and then used horribly. On what did she base her happiness? How did God try to bring her back and refocus her? What was He trying to show her?
2. Read James 1:2–4 and 1 Peter 1:3–9. What should our attitude be during suffering? Why does Peter tell us that suffering can be beneficial?
3. Read Paul's prayer in Ephesians 1:15–23. Write out everything he prays for the Ephesians. Notice that he doesn't mention their safety. His concern is for their hearts. Try to turn that prayer around and use it for yourself and those you love.

Chapter 4: God Whispers: "Am I Enough?"

1. Read through Psalm 63. In it, David praises God even while hiding from his enemies. How is David able to arrive at the point where he's happy just to be with God? How can you get there?
2. Read 1 Kings 18–19 and look at Elijah's experiences. In what way does your life mirror Elijah's? List all the ways that God comforted Elijah.

Chapter 5: God Whispers: "Do You Remember That You Are Dust?"

1. The following passages from the gospel of Mark show Jesus retreating—or at least trying to retreat—by Himself or with a small group of close friends. What prompted each retreat? What happened as a result? Read Mark 1:12–13; 1:35–39; 3:13; 6:30–33; 6:46; 7:24; 9:1–13; and 14:32–42.

2. What role should other people play in your healing? Read James 5:13–16 and Romans 12:3–16. Ask God to show you people in the body of Christ that you can go to for help, counsel, encouragement, and prayer.
3. Read Jeremiah 20:7–18. Jeremiah had been sent by God to preach to Israel, but he never won a convert. How do you think he felt? Why did he keep going? What did he say to God? How did God view Jeremiah—as a success or a failure?

Chapter 6: God Whispers: "Can I Carry You?"

1. Read through Psalm 40. What is David facing? In the same psalm, what does David tell us about his new song? What does David do now that he has that new song? Note that he still prays for his physical needs—he just knows that these are subordinate to his spiritual needs. What does he ask God for?
2. Read Matthew 11:28–30. What do you need rest from? What do these verses instruct us to do to find that rest? What would this look like in your own life?
3. Read Revelation 2:17 and think about the implications of your God-given new name, known at this time only to Him. What would that name be? Pray about it with God, and write your thoughts in a journal.

Chapter 7: God Whispers: "This Life Is Not All There Is"

1. Read through Paul's "heaven" passage in Philippians 3:12–21. Reading that, what do you think Paul was envisioning when he said, "living is Christ and dying is gain"? Knowing what you do about Paul, did it mean that he didn't care about life here on earth?
2. Read through Hebrews 12:1–3. Look at the context for verse 1. Who are the great cloud of witnesses? (Hint: take a look back through Chapter 11). What does this tell us about heaven? In this life, what is to be our focus?

3. Discuss the idea of "flashes" of joy that C.S. Lewis talks about, where you feel intimacy with Christ. Have you ever experienced it? Can you understand how joy and grief may be related?

4. How do we reconcile hoping for heaven but still also caring about this earth and its people today?

About the Author

Sheila Wray Gregoire speaks around North America urging women to trust that God is enough. An author of seven books and a syndicated parenting columnist, she started writing when her children were young and she wanted something to do from home. From those beginnings grew a blog that is viewed by several hundred thousand people a month, where she points people to the abundant life, and abundant relationships, God planned for us. Growing up in a single parent home gave her a passion to see marriages succeed, and together with her husband, Keith, she speaks at FamilyLife marriage conferences and other marriage outreaches.

She also is a sought after keynote speaker for women's events.

When she's not writing and speaking, you can find her at home in Belleville, Ontario, where she homeschools her two teenage daughters, and she knits. Even in line at the grocery store.

Find her at:

Blog: www.tolovehonorandvacuum.com

Facebook: www.facebook.com/sheila.gregoire.books

Twitter: www.twitter.com/sheilagregoire

Pinterest: www.pinterest.com/sheilagregoire

YouTube: www.youtube.com/sheilagregoire

If you would like to contact Sheila and share your story, she'd love to hear from you. She's also available to speak about how we can find shelter during even the worst storms. You can contact her at sheila@sheilawraygregoire.com.

Sheila Speaks

Sheila is available to speak at women's retreats, outreach events, and marriage events.

Her most popular talks and retreat packages include:

- **Extreme Makeover: Heart Edition.** (weekend retreat) Focusing on Philippians 3:4-14, Sheila looks at what it means to truly know Christ. In this retreat package, available as a 3-talk or 4-talk option, she walks through most of the information in this book.

- **Girl Talk: Straight Talk on Marriage and Intimacy.** (one-night event) Want a unique and exciting outreach for your church, while also providing your female members with encouragement and practical help? Sheila will present a humorous yet informative and challenging talk on what God designed sex for, why He designed marriage the way He did, and how we can help our marriages to thrive.

- **Leaving the Guilt Behind.** (one night event). Women feel perpetually guilty, largely because we hold ourselves up to such a high standard. Yet what is the root cause of this? Sheila looks at our "control freak" tendencies, and shares her testimony of how God taught her that ultimately our happiness and satisfaction is not found in looking like we have the perfect life, but instead in handing that life over to Him because He alone satisfies.

Other Books by Sheila Wray Gregoir

The Good Girl's Guide to Great Sex
By Sheila Wray Gregoire

Billions of people have had sex. Far fewer have made love. In *The Good Girl's Guide to Great Sex*, author Sheila Wray Gregoire helps women see how sexual intimacy was designed to be physically stupendous but also incredibly intimate.

Whether you're about to walk down the aisle or you've been married for decades, *The Good Girl's Guide to Great Sex* will lead you on a wonderful journey of discovery towards the amazing sex life God designed you for.

With humor, research, and lots of anecdotes, author Sheila Wray Gregoire helps women see how our culture's version of sex, which concentrates on the physical above all else, makes sex shallow. God, on the other hand, intended sex to unite us physically, emotionally, and spiritually. Gregoire walks through these three aspects of sex, showing how to make each amazing, and how to overcome the roadblocks in each area we often encounter.

Drawing on survey results from over 2,000 people, she also includes lots of voices from other Good Girls, giving insight into how other women have learned to truly enjoy sex in marriage.

"Like a funny big sister..." World Magazine
Published March 2012, Zondervan.

SHEILA WRAY GREGOIRE

the good girl's guide to great sex

(and you thought bad girls have all the fun)

FOREWORD by PAM FARREL

Other Books by Sheila Wray Gregoire

To Love, Honor, and Vacuum

"Sheila is about to challenge your thinking about your role as a wife and mother. I don't say that lightly. I read more advice about mothering and womanhood in a week than most people read in a year. But Sheila is on to something here."

—CARLA BARNHILL
Editor, *Christian Parenting Today*

"Reading this book provides a stimulus to do practical things to make life happier for everyone."

—CHRISTIAN OBSERVER

"Gregoire recognizes that for many women, housework isn't just housework. It's a source of deep anxiety, stress, and friction, but it doesn't have to be that way. If housework is driving you insane, you aren't alone."

—SAN DIEGO FAMILY

"Filled with spiritual wisdom and practical tips."

—KAREN STILLER
Associate Editor of *Faith Today* magazine

When you feel more like a
maid than a wife and mother

...to love,
honor,
and
vacuum

sheila wray gregoire

Foreword by Carla Barnhill, editor of Christian Parenting Today